Why write the land?

What does it mean to "write the land"?

How does the land write us?

Does our sense of place

inspire and inform

our art or is it

incidental?

41

of Alberta's

finest literary voices

explore these questions

with evocative poems that are as

compelling and diverse

as our landscape.

Writing the Land

Alberta through its poets

edited by

Dymphny Dronyk

and

Angela Kublik

House of Blue Skies
Edmonton, Alberta

ISBN-978-0-9784588-0-5

Printed by Red Pill Press, Grande Prairie, AB
Cover Design: Define Design, Grande Prairie, AB

Printed and bound in Canada
Published by House of Blue Skies
#74 10710-40 Avenue
Edmonton, AB T6J 2L8
Tel: 780-485-0521 Fax: 780-532-0921

akublik@blueskiespoetry.ca   www.blueskiespoetry.ca

In memory of Linda Smith,

who loved the land and walked on it with reverence.

We dedicate this anthology to all the artists out there

who pay attention and help us see.

Acknowledgements

Much gratitude goes to the talented fellows at Red Pill Press in Grande Prairie – without your savvy this book would still be just a daydream.

Our sincere appreciation extends to Eric Barstad of Shadow Box Creative Media who provides inexpensive web-hosting for blueskiespoetry.ca.

A thousand bows once again to Doug Wills, a true artist and gracious soul, for creating such a lovely cover.

Thank you to the Writer's Guild of Alberta, for being supportive of our adventure, and for graciously allowing us to latch onto the theme chosen for the 2007 conference – and for providing us with a venue to celebrate the launch of this book.

As always, we thank our families and all of our friends who have helped us along the way.

Finally, we are grateful for the support and wisdom of the gifted writers of Alberta.

CONTENTS

Introduction: Singing Canaries_____ 12

The Writer as Witness _____ *21*

Things I Will Give You: Landscape Makes A Promise
Deborah Lawson_____ 22
Moving Water
Deborah Lawson_____ 24
Wild Onions
Jenna Butler _____ 25
The Warp and Woof
Diane Buchanan _____ 26
The Quiet Gaze of Bison
Rosemary Griebel_____ 27
Sedoka
Richard Stevenson _____ 28
Henderson Lake Haiku
Richard Stevenson _____ 29
the offering
Catherine McLaughlin _____ 30
Crow in Grass
Tom Wayman_____ 32
Flute Song
Tom Wayman_____ 33
Chinook
John Bishop Ballem _____ 35
On Kerr's Prairie Skyes
Rob K. Omura _____ 36
losing Banff
Myrna Garanis _____ 38
high crime
Myrna Garanis _____ 39
Upper Kananaskis Lake
Barbara Janusz _____ 40
Mount Edith Cavell Suite
Pierrette Requier_____ 41
Islet Lake Trail
Anna Mioduchowska _____ 43
Noticed
Ian LeTourneau _____ 44

Weaslehead Variations

Stuart Ian McKay _____ 45

Christmas Visit

Blaine Newton _____ 47

Through Rose-Coloured Goggles

Jeananne Kathol Kirwin _____ 48

Urban Witness _____ *49*

To Have the Truth Seen and Recognized

Paul Pearson _____ 51

Three Haiku

Richard Stevenson _____ 52

Interstice 1

Catherine Owen _____ 53

Interstice 22

Catherine Owen _____ 54

Interstice 25

Catherine Owen _____ 55

what we don't see

Wendy Joy _____ 56

Unravelled

Pierrette Requier _____ 58

The Elk Island Park Expedition, April 2004

Ben Murray _____ 60

Homeland Security

Joanne Underwood _____ 62

Reverence _____ *65*

Revelation

Diane Buchanan _____ 66

Walking Meditation

Audrey J. Whitson _____ 67

a prayer to peace

Greg Schmidt _____ 69

After the Storm, Banff National Park

Anna Mioduchowska _____ 70

The Teeth of Nose Hill

Vivian Hansen _____ 71

November in the Wilderness Park

Marlene Dean _____ 72

worship

Catherine McLaughlin _____ 74

Indelible ———————————— *77*

It is a big

Margaret Macpherson _____ 78

Pump Jacks

Ian LeTourneau _____ 80

Cutline.

A.G. Boss _____ 81

Live Earth

Vivian Demuth _____ 83

Faders

Vivian Demuth _____ 84

Hoo Doos Trail

Brenda Leifso _____ 85

Saturday, Waiting Outside the Recording Studio Barn

Carol MacKay ———————————— 87

Our Imprint on the Land _____ *88*

Seasons

Marion Brooker _____ 90

Touching Trees

Vivian Hansen _____ 91

Pete's Dilemma

Richard Stevenson _____ 92

Near Milk River, looking for the Sweetgrass Hills

Weyman Chan _____ 93

October

Diane Buchanan _____ 95

winter highway

Jenna Butler _____ 97

Not Every Highway Has a Number

Tom Wayman _____ 98

Driving the 22

Brenda Leifso _____ 100

Sketches of a Return, February 2006

Pierrette Requier _____ 102

The Land's Imprint on Us _____ *105*

this landscape

Kathy Fisher _____ 106

Dominion of Wind

Deborah Lawson _____ 107

Great Lone Land
Rob K. Omura _____ 109
At the Frank Slide Interpretative Centre
Rob K. Omura _____ 111
on the brink of the slide
Barbara Janusz _____ 113
Blowing at the Sky
Anna Mioduchowska _____ 114
Finders Keepers
Ben Murray_____ 116
Drumheller
Kerry Mulholland _____ 118

Born from the Land _____*120*
An Anthem
Marion Brooker _____ 121
Vast Prairie Puja
Gayle Sacuta _____ 122
Where Are You From?
Gayle Sacuta _____ 123
Scandinavian Picnic at Markerville
Carol MacKay _____ 124
Farmhouse, Castor
Jenna Butler _____ 125
Clam Digging in the Battle River
Rosemary Griebel_____ 126
Power of the Land
Susan Picard _____ 127
Selling the Family Farm
Carol MacKay _____ 128
Grandpa Moves the Hay
Cheryl King _____ 129
The Last Days of Mrs. Allen
Steven Michael Berzensky _____ 132
Grandfathers
Andy Michaelson _____ 135
Connect the Dots
Bob Stallworthy _____ 137

Afterword: Putting Writing in its Place _____138
Contributors _____142
About the Editors _____154

Introduction

Singing Canaries

Angela and I had long mused and schemed about publishing an anthology. Over the years the reality of undertaking such a huge project discouraged us. One of us would almost be convinced to leap, gleefully teetering on the edge – and then the other would pull her back, citing wise and logical reasons such as expense, time commitment, the dire and financially unrewarding state of publishing in Alberta.

But as time passed we honed our experiences as writers and editors and technology changed enough to improve our odds. Thanks to Sam Montgomery of Red Pill Press in Grande Prairie we learned that these days, a book can be published professionally and affordably.

"Leap and a safety net shall appear" the saying goes. When we revisited the idea of doing a book this spring we jumped blissfully into the blue sky that shimmered beyond the cliff's edge. It was serendipitous and felt right. Many of the writers we knew were talking about the "power of the land," about what it means to "write the land" and we knew – finally – what the theme of our anthology *had* to be. The land had a constant voice in our own writing. The anthology was a way to gather voices together, to create a chorus – whether in celebration or in mourning we did not know.

At first our outrageous idea seemed pretty safe. Angela posted the call on her fledgling website, www.blueskiespoetry.ca, and we waited. "Who would even hear about our call for submissions?" we joked. And who would take it seriously if they did? Did "writing the land" matter to any other Alberta writers or just to us? But as poems began to float in, at first one every few days, then a few each day our hope grew. The quality and diversity of the work was astounding.

It is easy to edit when you can quickly spot the weaker submissions. You put them aside and concentrate on the stronger pieces. For us this was not the case. We thought the submissions would dry up. We thought maybe the brilliant poets were also the keeners, organized enough to submit well before deadline. But the vibrant, passionate words just kept coming. It was exhilarating. And overwhelming – because then we had to make our choices, and later on find ways to weave those words into a tapestry where the warp and the weft were in harmony.

Finally we asked each contributor to respond to two critical questions. We needed to understand the context in which the poems had been created. We did not want to assume that our contributors were inspired to "write the land" for the same reasons that we did.

"What does 'writing the land' mean to you?" we asked. "What thoughts can you share with us about the responsibility writers have to the land?" Once again the response from the writers was deeply moving and affirmed our purpose.

Some of our contributors felt that writers have the same responsibility as any other human being – no more, no less. Some felt that the unique role of writers is to describe the land with integrity so that the reader may see it with new eyes. For many, writing the land took on spiritual or political dimensions. Two poets likened the role of writers to the canaries in the coalmines.

Words such as honesty and reverence, paying attention, "getting it right," having a sense of place, of being written by the land showed up time and again in their answers:

> "I think the land writes us – dirt in our pores, sun lining the skin." - *Brenda Leifso*

> "I think all writers consciously or unconsciously write from a sense of place. If the writer is fortunate to have a strong connection to the land it is that geography that will inform their writing and that landscape

that they will bring to life." - *Rosemary Griebe*l

"I'm a born and raised Albertan, I have never lived anywhere else. In a way I still don't understand, this place and my experience of it finds its way into everything I write. I'm still surprised to encounter people who think this land (Alberta, all of Canada for that matter) is boring and unsuitable as subject matter for any kind of art. My job as a prairie poet is to find life and give life to the experience of this place, not somewhere far off." - *Stuart Ian McKay*

"[The writer's responsibility is] no different than anyone else. We are not the keepers of the land in any moral or mystic sense. We can be chroniclers, in much the same way as a painter or photographer." - *Blaine Newton*

"So perhaps our unique responsibility, as writers and poets, is to rekindle a sense of wonder about the land and to encourage people to seek a more intimate, respectful and joyful relationship with it." - *Deborah Lawson*

"For me as a writer much of the wild--places and species--are disappearing. In some cases, now and in years to come, our words may be the only witnesses of what *is*. It is important that we pay attention." - *Audrey J. Whitson*

"We owe a debt to the landscapes that shape us. We need to dig deep for an honest core in our writing about the land, even if it's hard to get to that honest place." - *Wendy Joy*

"The land is integral to my person. My voice is informed by the Prairie. The land is the foundation of my reality. Any responsibility I have to self must also extend to the land. Respect, concern, appreciation, stewardship."
- Gayle Sacuta

"Being open to the incredible landscape that surrounds us, and gaining inspiration from its beauty, strength, and history. It also means being cognizant of what is happening to the land in the present, both positive and negative, and striving through words to protect the land for the coming generation. It's not a one-way relationship -- we don't get to draw inspiration for free." - *Jenna Butler*

"I think it's important to be honest about the state of one's own backyard and to point out the special-ness of ordinary places. There seems to be a prevalent notion that because we have preserved some of Alberta's wilderness areas, that the rest of the land, primarily rural, is fair game for oil & gas development at the expense of agriculture, wildlife and the environment. Writers can offer an alternative view." - *Carol MacKay*

"As Albertans and as Canadians, an integral part of our identity is our connection with the land. This authentic connection is often denigrated by sectors of society who see the land as "resource" to be used to make money.

It's important that writers give voice to their love of the land for its own sake, and that they empower their readers by fostering the idea that a personal connection with nature is not only legitimate but crucial to our survival as whole human beings." - *Marlene Dean*

"If all citizens are called upon to share our time, talent and treasure to preserve the land and to become a friend to our environment, then artists may best show good stewardship through our skills of perception and expression, and the goodwill that rises from the pleasure of creating and sharing our art. If this is so, then writers have a calling to protect and preserve the land and our environment through the many tools of language." - *Jeananne Kathol Kirwin*

"For me, being raised aware of '*la terre*', the soil, meant knowing that it has the last word, that it needs to be related to. For my grandparents it meant survival, for my parents, working hard to improve the quality of life for their children, and for me it means not forgetting the source of our daily bread." - *Pierrette Requier*

"Writers, like everyone else, need to forego ingrained antediluvian beliefs whereby the land is exploited, taken for granted, and/or regarded as a glorified dump for all our crap, most of which we don't need. I suppose the best writers can do is remind us of our primal connection to this fragile world we're despoiling faster than a speeding SUV.

Perhaps in this regard writers are the canaries whose song will hopefully be heard over the crash and burn of the coal mines falling all around us." - *Ben Murray*

"We have a tremendous responsibility because a writer has the ability to stir emotions or to put forward an idea. Imagination can move mountains. Words can make people stop and think." - *Rob K. Omura*

"If my poetry opens the eyes and the ears of my audience to something in their natural environment they have either not noticed before, or have not considered worthy of attention, if I succeed in transferring even a fraction of my own wonder, I will go to sleep a happy poet." - *Anna Mioduchowska*

Diane Buchanan sent a poem to answer our questions, of which we share an excerpt here:

Let me walk this earth singing
for the Dodo and the dinosaur,
the snow leopard and the sparrow,
the orca and the orang-utan,
the polar bear and the piping plover,
the disappeared and the disappearing.

Let me walk this earth in prayer
for only then will I find my way.
Let me walk this earth with reverence
for every step taken leaves
a footprint behind.

We hope these poems inspire you to slow down and pay attention, to let the land write itself under your skin, to walk with reverence, to join your own voice in our chorus of this land, Alberta, with all its loveliness, its riches, and its paradoxes.

Dymphny Dronyk & Angela Kublik

The Writer as Witness

"Alive with the germ of inspiration"

Rob K. Omura,
Excerpt from:
On Kerr's Prairie Skyes

Deborah Lawson

Things I Will Give You: Landscape Makes A Promise

I will give you green
in its hundred shades,
from the barest hint
threaded along the growing golden stalk,
to the near-black shadow
caught between thick spruce needles

I will give you light,
the hard-edged morning's
etched exposure focused
through dew's magnifying glass,
and the flat, direct burning of noon,
and this afternoon amber,
flowing ever lower over
the lush and liquid grid of these fields.

I will give you brushwork,
from sweeping and generous
to delicate and precise,
painting these contoured hills
onto flat prairie canvas,
where they rise
like a spirit uplifting.

I will give you the sound
of many wild hands clapping,
the echoing applause of the hills.
But when ecstasy
gives way to deep listening
you will recognize the sound
of your own wild heart,

22

Deborah Lawson

echoing the heartbeat of the land,
the parallel sighs and undulations
of your own chambers of wonder,
a gallery where the masterwork
of this sweet landscape will live
as long as you do, as long
as your memory beats.

Deborah Lawson

Moving Water

Prominent silver. You transform
midnight's moonlight into the blood of the land.

Between river banks you capture
the lightning flash of shooting stars.

Your dance extends
high above your frothing frenzy,
laces the leaping crests of moving water
with spicy ozone, a pulmonary elixir
that penetrates the lungs.

A circulation system, vast, connective,
you carry my canoe along life-giving capillaries,
permit the encroachment of one small intruder
infiltrating the giant heart of a giant land.

Jenna Butler

Wild Onions

creek ducks the boundary fence
leaves it slackjawed & dangling
spring   the cattle
wallow in runoff mud
play their spines along the wire

up the coulee
ironstone peters to cactus
wild lupine

the onions are found
by scent   bite
of trodden leaves
    bulbs unearthed like molars
    crepuscular canyon light

wild taste of
earth & dark water

coyote on a lip of land   ochre
moon saddling predawn sky

Diane Buchanan

The Warp and Woof

Grass is the cloth of the prairies,
a pattern of roots woven underground.
In darkness threads of fescue,
vetch, old man's whiskers,
needle and spear, porcupine,
brome and bluegrass twine
and entwine to bind
the earth together. Grass

emerges like the tip of an iceberg
in a land too dry for forests,
too wet for desert, shows
only its hair. On the surface,
foliage, flowers, blades
and seeds while beneath,
so much unseen,
so much unknown.

Rosemary Griebel

The Quiet Gaze of Bison

The quiet gaze of bison,
mouths moving
over fescue
and milkweed,
sway of wind on throat latch
and bull's beard.
Dark, ancient ghosts
shifting over the land.

On this bleached prairie
beyond the salt flats
of Sullivan Lake
the small light
of a torch
on a cave wall
at Lascaux
still gleams in their eyes.

Richard Stevenson

Sedoka

Crawling into cracks
of the old garden timbers,
the bees carry rolled up leaves.

Blueprints for a nest
or apian wallpaper?
The plans are still green

Richard Stevenson

Henderson Lake Haiku

Coals to Newcastle –
a paper wasp with green plans
in a rolled leaf

*

branch almost fully
turbanned by the wasp nest –
one apple protrudes

Catherine McLaughlin

the offering

I first saw her as I walked
along the gravel road
out by the wheat fields
something drew my eye

shrouded in dust, cradled
by bleached grasses
feathers muddy and broken
she is silent
though her black bill
remains open

her skull is hollow now
empty sockets a tunnel
for the light

in death's dance
outside is in
where her neck once curved
beads of bone
necklace
her brown and
speckled feathers

I kneel to look
more closely, then
touch her

these bones are cool
smooth like shells
feathers soft
under my fingers

Catherine McLaughlin

then I see
what caught my eye
as the afternoon sun
finds her

still offering a flash
of mallard green

Tom Wayman

Crow in Grass

Atop green June blades
out of which myriad dandelions
forest, each tiny trunk hoisting
its white globe of seeds,

stalk three crows. The nearest
pistons head and neck as she paces,
eyes swiveling left and right

to secure the wildness
these beaks bring.

Tom Wayman

Flute Song

Three winds
braid through me

Three winds:
One the body's petulances

exaltations of joy, moods
from quietude to

domineering, even a willingness
to inflict pain--an allegiance

vowed to that capo
the Murderer

Three winds:
Also, a day that inches by

minute after minute
to construct years become leaves pouring from

a yellowed aspen
in late Fall

--an unceasing gale
that reshapes flesh like steam

that rattles downspouts, windows
a brute flow

Tom Wayman

that disperses chimney smoke downwards and away
along with entire forests

blocks of stores
neighbors, parents

Three winds:
And one the stream of ashes from a burn pile

swirling with me as I circle
to try to escape the particulates that

scratch at the eyes
choke my airway

confuse me about which body, whose time
I move inside

about who pushes forward through the
gusts and eddies

with my name

John Bishop Ballem

Chinook

"Snow Eater" the Blackfoot call you.
Born of the sea,
Flowing inland
To warm the land,
Climb a mountain
And bestow
A benediction of rain
On the forest below.
Chill and dry
At the top.
Nearly touching the sky.
Warmed by the speed
Of your descent,
You blow through
The Clouds,
Carving an arch
High in the sky.
Your signature.
Then march
Across the foothills
Raising the temperature,
Melting ice and snow
As you go.

Rob K. Omura

On Kerr's *Prairie Skyes*

Elephantine skies
weigh down prairie flatlands
where sagebrush swats at
grainy memories,
kicked up with each step
like black flies
let loose from a peaty ditch.

A fine ochre of yellow and brown dust
blows hot over the stalks and straw of
an endless sea of wheat.
It salts my face and hair,
the grit gets under my shirt
and chaffs my chest.

If you follow the curved horizon
study sextant and compass
hold your course Magellan-sure
telescope your eyes
through the haze of heat waves,
you can make out a red grain elevator
adrift like the doomed Medusa on goldenrod seas,
it yaws in a nor'easter
tired floor boards groan and tiller
twists in the wind.

From a dipped wet tip
drawn up from a spring creek
hidden in the footprint
of a coulee
cobalt skies fill the canvas

Rob K. Omura

wet with thunderheads
pregnant with promise,
alive with the germ of inspiration.

Earth and blue sky hold
an uneasy truce
in this border town
alone in a nameless plain.

I know this place.
I, too, drew awe
from the cold well
buried deep in the sepia-coloured
silt of nostalgia, drowning.
I, too, held my breath
to hear the hush
when the rushing wind
whispered my name.

Myrna Garanis

losing Banff

mountain markers abound, at least we're in the vicinity,
so near and yet so far is the song we're not singing,
on this second wrong turnoff of a shortening afternoon

despite the map's precision, despite having been before,
we cannot correct our course
'no U-turn' one sign declares, too late,
we've overshot a major mountain town,
trip after trip, same promise to keep, a sharper eye,
not for bear who sometimes stumble out
of hibernation, mistaken in the date; nor for elk,
we have plenty of postcards

in the crosswind, two ravens pedal backwards,
they should have tipped us off that roads
can be deceitful, mountain roads most of all,
built to bypass normal melt routes, built to skirt,
to cheat, to cut off miles, mere travelers are bound
to lose their way, fated to repeat the mistake

Myrna Garanis

high crime
Banff, Alberta

February greys down by six,
climbers comment on the longer light,
they forget the patient progress
over December and January,
two stolid minutes daily

clouds parade past chalets
in flagrant imitation
of the slippery slopes below,
clear case of copyright invasion

clouds horn in, persist
in their infringement
of the privacy of peaks,
attempt to move mountains,
delay the seeping light

Rundle next to Norquay
rub shoulders with
the down-darkening sky.
everyone plays at camouflage,
mountains claiming to be clouds,
clouds claiming to be mountains,
deceit on all three sides

Barbara Janusz

Upper Kananaskis Lake

shimmering green-blue, emeralds cut into sapphires
white caps rise in gusts, undulating heat
receding glacier clings to rock overhang
tree line advances
- a mirage of creeping forward.

"*Pas trop chaud, pas trop chaud,*"
father placates offspring, shrouded from head to foot
in trousers, long-sleeved shirts, visored caps
approach water's edge *avec trepidation.*
As if irradiating solar light
could conspire with glacial lake
to scorch exposed skin
as if mirage might defy itself
blink of an eye
deluge of glacial ice, water
cup running over
as in biblical times, legendary Noah constructed ark
from timber felled in collapsed glacier's path.

grey granite rocks punctuate clay bed
some splintered, sharp as serrated knife
flat skipping stones break waves
green blades of grass sparsely take hold.

Pierrette Requier

Mount Edith Cavell Suite

1

Ice Age rolls in hard-hatted driving a bulldozer,
provokes rock-slides as She rams, dislodges,
scoops up and deposits at whim huge stone chunks,
shakes and shoves boulder-sized pieces of mountain.

2

She the mighty frozen one flies high
spans ridges forty meters deep, wears Angel wings.
From engorged tips thunders down avalanches as
her pelvis roars and throbs.

3

Sun follows Her, faithfully returns   returns   returns
shines on over summits   melts snow   slow-snakes
running water down mountain flanks.

4

And here and here and here   still She sifts
sifts and shuffles more snow   sifts it like flour
in the bowl of her great dream.
Then like a drunken cantankerous gambler
She shakes the die again and again, lusts after the windfall.
Like a rock hound she rattles her tumbler
clunk on clunk, dry dead thuds, as stumbling stones
grind and crush rock rock rock
rockrockrocks to silt as splash washes   washes.

Pierrette Requier

5

Sun stoops to Her, nibbles glacier's toe,
rises and kisses her forehead, sculpts ice caves,
caresses with breath her skin, makes perfect aqua waves
transmutes iceberg shapes with his lavish sensuous
tongue, fills her round pool.

Ice recedes.

Anna Mioduchowska

Islet Lake Trail

Handful of wild hazelnuts
the only hard evidence of late September,
a place, where time had lost consciousness for a day
instead of hours
loosened thoughts
winding
through an artistic catastrophe, paints
spilled in the night by a naughty child,
delirium of little fingers
"look Ma! look!"

In a smudge of light,
                    an elegant squiggle,
garter snake, suspended
between prime blue, and green
fading to earth.

Ian LeTourneau

Noticed

We may not have noticed in the day's blur,
ten hours of hiking, looking up mostly, vistas
of blue. We may not have noticed
if it weren't for this simple picture,
taken by a friend, who happened to stop,
and because some happenstance thing
like light struck him, snapped it.
Perhaps only ten square feet of earth,
where roots of spruce and pine overlap,
connecting rows of trees in a vast disorderly
network, worn from the slow workings
of weather and hiking boots. Needles, moss,
twigs sifted and shifted on top.

There must be some will of seed, having blown
this way, settled on this order, having frisked
for fertile soil in the sub-alpine air.

Though we all stopped to look at the first flowers
of the year, glacier lilies nodding
their drooping yellow heads,
we passed right by the interlocking sturdiness
of these trees. And because it was
ordinary, went unnoticed.

Stuart Ian McKay

Weaslehead Variations

one

of a morning in march, immediate, as if the lichen encrusted
on cold, rough stone were the same as the beaten open bark
of trees; the last snow that huddles over the green, even
alive, moss the same as the sky; this little spot of earth,
the only voice here, the expanse, in locked land placidity

two

thick sheets of ice white on the waking river, thawing the
thin lines snapping, gradual for weeks over the moving
water, of ice scraping against ice, the river's edge, there, the
rocks the vastness of its flowing isolated in caught branches,
leaves, soil

three

mud at river bank, gully; dry on hills, plains, expectant,
alive, to widening thickets, heaviness of stones, held in
the presence of tiny footed things, birds, mice, deer, bear
and others; blown exposed to sun, wind; or rain weighted
burdened down as if itself the cause, the root, the being

Stuart Ian McKay

four

but the breeze loosening their unmistakable essence,
deepened boundaries of drying yellowing grasses, unyielding
wet brown leaves in places let open to the sun, in others the
embraced layers of seven months of snow resistant
still, giving away, as in waiting for months further on

five

high branched rustle of crow, magpie wing against aspen
poplar, pine; song at counterpoint with blackness clash
dark, dark brown feathers, eyes, as the stain of soil, shadows
on the below valley, the pathways, suddenly flying over ice

six

shine toppled trees roots gesturing exposed and worn down
in the intimacy of river, wind, seasons, as the wrinkles
around a woman's eyes are to the land itself touched
tenderly, even to the formed spaces where anchoring roots
ache in the remembered river bank soil, defying birds,
leaving footsteps venial, as if to say an eternal thing was

Blaine Newton

Christmas Visit

Cold air scratching my lungs
bare branches clawing the
red cloud sky.
To fall here so far
from anyone
I would be dead before
the low sun had buried
itself beneath the scrub
trees of the distant hedgerow.

Drifts shelter tilting stones
holding them against the wind
time freezing in this white
openness
distance and time above me
like the sun-dogs that breathe in
the steam of my breath.

When I can no longer look
into the whiteness
aware of the stiffness
the creeping death
in my joints
I fight my way back past
the church
gunshot steps through
the crusted drifts.

Jeananne Kathol Kirwin

Through Rose-Coloured Goggles

Above the winter-worn lodgepole pines
Whose indigo shadows dapple the bright whiteness,
We soar in the lift
Toward the heavens so
Drenched, their blueness might drip.
Numb toes, frost-nipped fingertips,
Wind whooshing in our ears, whir
Of pulleys, the give of crisp snow under skis.

I gaze upward through rose-coloured goggles
Toward splayed red rays.
Through clouded eyes I glimpse the haze below me,
Tucked pink and soft among folded grey peaks.
Then I see the dark jut of jagged rock,
Straining, scraping against the saturation
Of the cerulean sky.

Urban Witness

"Where does the land end?"

Joanne Underwood
Excerpt from: Homeland Security

Paul Pearson

To Have the Truth Seen and Recognized

sideways six hours
from noon this light this late
fall sunset lasts half
the day

to the careless eye
everything is brown but
smaller spectrums catch
the sun pushing through thickening
air in tricks of gold, amber,
copper

in the city
we don't notice the sun
all light is street
light interstitial and weak
mountains are wired with a switch
between the binaries I've never
seen the red in your hair so
clearly

Richard Stevenson

weeping birch branches
flounce in an august squall –
I miss the yield sign

*

blue light through the trees –
distant campfire beckoning?
no, big screen TV

*

boundless blue sky –
empty manuscript staves
of black power lines

Catherine Owen

Interstice 1

Everywhere here – vestiges and markers, on the earth
what goes on under – Epcor
cupping its tumuli above the White Mud
in the park with its even trees, posts
and on each, signs emblazoning pipelines –
beneath your feet – oil. In this place, be
careful where you dig – the polished clasps of houses
weaken and into fissures spill children on bicycles, spoil
tidy white dogs, all the hardwood, all the fixtures, and the wind
is always riffling the black river where it lips into grasses,
shimmers in the northern Prairie sun a long dark door in the land.

Catherine Owen

Interstice 22

No snow left
- end of April
but on the darkest slopes
of Fort Edmonton Park
grass dazzling up
green
except a five foot patch on the lawn
where the failed
ice rink
melted to a brown drench
the school buses
audacious as dandelions
buzzing by on 44th
and a jackrabbit
feasting on weeds
in the newly revealed
garden
spotted now with dun,
uncamouflaged & fragile
in the sunshine.

Catherine Owen

Interstice 25

Snow in May and then – sudden –
heat wave a week after.
Spring this blowsy convergence of lilacs,
apple blossoms – a few days and the wind splats it
into the yard.
Mosquitoes hatch, too fast for your forgetfulness of blood
and your flesh is planets.
From the highest mountain ash branch, a
robin chirrups like ice – all else a desert in the throat,
crashed sapped beneath the fan,
no time to grow accustomed to the sun.
Punching its golden fist through the sky.

Wendy Joy

what we don't see

I like my garden half-wild.
Everything in my small vegetable patch melds
tomato plants gone crazy, lettuce and mint co-mingle, carrots hide.
In September, on a night with sudden frost,
I'll be out with bowls and buckets, and flashlight,
searching for tomatoes in every dark plant cranny.
But now it is August and their fruit hangs green and heavy,
one tomato turning orange on the vine.

I stay out so late weeding, deadheading, watering,
that the half-moon rises in greeting.
All children are in, even birds are still,
the neighbourhood magpies bedded down for the night.
The clouds alter as the sun leaves them, making a slow change
from white to grey in the deepening sky.
Scent rises most from white flowers,
and the dusk carries the smell of ornamental onions,
their starburst globes rising on stiff spikes,
and tall German Stattice, with tiny pink-white blooms
on many reaching fingers, waving and moving with the breeze.
They glimmer in the dark, a gift for our eyes that seek light,
see light for so long, even when it is gone from us.

My sunflowers are eight feet tall, leaves broader than a platter.
Giants above my children, sometimes they've grown six inches in a day,
hurrying to get to sky. Now they finally bloom and give everything
to the flower, huge yellow discs growing wider and fatter each day.
Bees and dragonflies have gotten stuck in the stamens, trapped, doomed
to slow death by bloom, legs held fast by developing seeds.
The bee surely yearning for the hive, the noise, the smell of her sisters.

The clouds move and keep moving, the night is never still.
The absence of sun allows the smell of earth, bloom, wetness.
Then the moon rises and the clouds change again.

I garden so late I can't see the water entering the flower beds,
have to listen to the earth tell me when it has had enough.

Wendy Joy

And I watch the stars come out. They are always there anyway,
waiting, even when we are blind to them.
Like the bee, we don't see what we don't see.
Our eyes search the shadows for light, always. In this night sky,
the clouds might seem to slowly disappear, but they remain.
The bee might survive the night, pull cold legs out once morning mist
wets her yellow leg-hold trap. I might wake to find her gone,
seeking home, rest, repair, with an amazing story of survival,
courage in the face of it all, held fast on the pinnacle of the world,
till fingers loosened and she pulled herself away.

Pierrette Requier

Unravelled

Ravel's String Quartet in f
second movement
inches me down and across
to the North Side,
already late for a deadline.
Winter slept in this year,
just woke up to its shifty business
of snow-blowing snow,
car exhaust spewing fast and
furious as the wind gusts.
Flashing brake lights
the only flick-flick
of colour in this blustery
end of winter morning.
Grey sky hung over the river valley
with its stick trees: bare poplars, sober spruce
prissy pines, and its bottle-necked wet road.
At the bottom of the hill
staid, stoic traffic lights
do their old fashioned work.
Green waves a slushy go,
amber flits one more car through,
red holds a gloved hand up.
And the river -
that brought settlement here
in the first place -
meanders on
its cold course.
Here on its banks
we still huddle, try to keep warm
eight months of the year.

Pierrette Requier

Here where we have sprawled.
Hard to call this home
to have the heart for it
on this March morning.

Ben Murray

The Elk Island Park Expedition, April 2004

our car is no sled-dog driven ice breaker
catching its breath, breathing new world air;
our skin does not erupt
in the red wake of Amazonian ants

and yet, we get lost

making a right instead of a left
our destination waves bye in the rear-view,
fill 'er up the wishful phrase pacing
the tense gas-gauging miles

fortunately, a gas station appears
no mirage, engine purring
with the promise of unleaded
we finally find our place
next to idling families
fuelling this Sunday with butane fires
and holiday smiles, smoke signalling
the envious, forgotten city

it's a day of kites crowding
cormorants' air space, of bleached
lakeshore trails tanning
in the intermittent sun,
of playgrounding adults
kidding time

dusk arrives and it's so quiet
we imagine hearing bison breathe,
their hulking masses just standing there--

Ben Murray

are they watching us in the dimming light?
our watches only really start ticking
after dark, when it's time to go

the only ones left in the park
we hear coyotes and owls lullaby
northern lights,
our flashlight's paltry beam
upstaged by the sky

we make our way past recent plops
of elk and bison, each dry step a relief
to exploring soles

and there is the car, the last
in the lot, the click of its ignition signals
a successful expedition,
of a safe return

Joanne Underwood

Homeland Security

I notice the sky first

where does land end   sky begin?

I've come from Singapore   jungle city   rain trees and shortened views
look up and all you see are branches   look down and find hibiscus
bougainvillea   lush greenery   rust red soil

but I've come home   home to Alberta
teen years in Cold Lake   with that bigbig sky
    undulating and popping with sounds of northern lights in winter
university years in Edmonton   riverbanks   ring roads   riding the bus
birthing years in Calgary   Rockies waiting just over there

yet it's the sky I notice first   bluewide   cloudless   in my line of sight
    through all 360 degrees

when I look down I'm surprised at how green it all is   remember sere
    brown
this Calgary is beautiful   early April
no time yet for dryness which might come later
which does come later

I learn to xeriscape   mulch garden beds with rocks or bark
keep in precious moisture

I plant native trees   softgreen larch which don't seem to mind clay soil
    the lack of nutrients
and grasses   prairie grasses and wildflowers   stunning in their beauty

I walk in Fish Creek Park   see deer   coyotes   signs of beavers

Joanne Underwood

our wild rose   pretty little plant   ubiquitous along river pathways
tells me there's beauty amidst clay and rock

a visit to Waterton Lakes National Park reveals more
spectacular rare flowers   flashy foreground to mountain silhouettes

I realize this land is no poor cousin   this land is Home

Reverence

*"I tell you
 this is a place
for worship"*

Catherine McLaughlin
Excerpt from: worship

Diane Buchanan

Revelation

I've passed this slough everyday
on my walk around this country
block. It's hard to ignore,
though I have, too busy
wading in my own marshy thoughts, until –
one day I see gold.
A blackbird with a bright yellow head.
I can't resist. I stop to kneel, to be
still, to be one with the grass on the shore and
I look, I really look. Time floats away
among the rushes, the reeds rising in wind tickled water.
Beyond flat fields of grain and all around me, sky,
half my world filled with that huge blue prairie sky. Here,
at the slough it is spring. There are red-winged
as well as yellow-headed blackbirds, a pair
of geese, dragon flies, ducks of all colors, shapes and sizes.
I want to know their names, to be able to call them
all by name. Everything is flutter,
flash and flurry. The air pulses as fertility bursts
into croaky song. I breathe in
moist scent of citreous, feel the earth
throb beneath my knees, now damp where
slough has touched me.

How can I not be awed?
How can I not be prayerful?
How can I not wonder
if I am kneeling at
the threshold of a temple?

Audrey J. Whitson

Walking Meditation
     for Thich Nhat Hanh

Dimly we know the mystery
in the deadfall that supports us:
                     the life in this place, they told us,
                     is on the ground.

                          Journal Entry, March 25, 1995
                              Slave Lake, Alberta

Finding a forest
older than yourself
you widen a clearing inside.
Listen through your toes.
You'll hear openings

created long before we conceived
stainless steel corridors.
Fine white hair of fungi
grown tough with use,
whose nodules carried nitrogen

long before we knew
the simplest chemical equations.
Penetrate the layers of debris
foresters call decadence.
Let your feet caress

the round greenness swelling
each measured step
a Devonian incarnation.

Audrey J. Whitson

Know the tubers that spread
with fibrous veins a thousand times

more intricate than the blue
on the back of your hand. Press
the pockets of balsam on the fir.
Essence of a life force,
origins we cannot fathom.

Greg Schmidt

a prayer to peace

come join me in my pagan, pantheistic rituals
we shall worship mother earth in all her glory
and dance naked under the full moon
we will drink fully of this earthly existence
as if this here were of utmost importance
as if we could actually experience heaven on earth
and walk in god's glory along the way
we shall live as though each one of us is worthy of god's grace
no matter where we were born or what we believe
only to be judged by what we do, how we live our life
then truly shall we walk in god's grace
and experience heaven on earth.
                    Amen.

Anna Mioduchowska

After the Storm, Banff National Park

Day after the storm, the mountains
dig themselves out, clear their ears, noses,
spruces shudder under the new weight,
the raven, sober again, flies in a straight line.

It's twenty below.
The sun scrubs the sky with child-like gusto,
the slopes furry, bears dozing after a good meal.
Great-great-grandma invented God on a day like this,
an excuse to lift up her voice *ave ave*
gloria in excelsis!

A few steps forward, then back.
I study the imprints left in the snow.
Such distinct stride.
Who was it that walked this way –
a woman of wisdom?
feather brain?

My thumb, the ink in my pen, frozen, I move on.
The shadow leading me flaps its arms
in an attempt to fly; fingers cum wing tip feathers,
large hooded head, clunky torso, it's an owl on stilts,
followed by a two-legged camera,
each step a walk-through photo.

Solitary cloud lingers over a valley plush
with a billion trees,
welcome rest after the push 'n shove.
Two gray wolves rub their flanks
against my shin in search of a good word,
I take the pen out of my mouth.

Vivian Hansen

The Teeth of Nose Hill

these calloused sandstone outcroppings
are the teeth of Nose Hill
grinning, the whorls of stone chain linking
past, and watermarks meandering

like logos
stretching
your hands and arms across the grainy surface
then   lift off your skin, tattooed with sandstone braids
etched into the hull of you,

refusing comfort in your skin,
you sit upon its surface
surf the rock, smooth, massage the stone against your palms
levitate the wonder

Marlene Dean

November in the Wilderness Park

We walked in the wilderness park
on a warm November afternoon
and you said
"You can see why poets compare these hills to the body of a
woman."
And I could.
I could see the soft textures and flesh toned curves,
the shadowed folds harbouring life–
the large eared mule deer,
watchful and curious.

We followed an animal trail up a hill where it opened
onto a meadow of thick fescue, gold in the autumn light
and you said,
"This is wealth!"
We sat in the sheltered bowl for a long while,
our faces warmed by the sun
and then, silent as churchgoers we walked down again.

Along the river valley dead leaves clung to grey branches
and rattled like dry bones in the breeze.
The shadows of the hills grew longer and spread overland
like a black tide.

Out of the corner of my eye I see a black dog
running beside me, a black dog, long and sleek,
noiseless as nightfall,
a black dog, keeping his steady pace.

We came, at last, to a cliff
where an expanse of river was framed by the bare branches

Marlene Dean

of a giant cottonwood tree and
shored in the distance by the sensuous hills,
and you said,
"This is how it was for the pioneers.
Can you imagine?
If you lived here you would have everything you needed–
a good source of water and fertile land to grow your food."

And I imagine a life full with the sound of moving water
and the cries of hawk and owl.
I imagine a life rich with the smell of earth
and I imagine love
then, as now,
chased by the black dog of November.

Catherine McLaughlin

worship

I'll tell you what I saw
I'll tell you I saw light
dancing by the river

first the sun shot through
the black branches of that maple
laid out blue shadows
on the snow near the church
so I followed

deer tracks led me down
a trail - narrow, lined with red willow
thin whips springing as I passed
just above the river shining pewter
cold and sweet to my lips
when I bent to taste

then I turned, found the inlet
almost frozen
ice hooding the shore

late day sun beamed
over the hill
shone low across the water
caught ice flaked on its edge
and began the dance

Catherine McLaughlin

did I pray, you ask
I was on my knees
in the snow, staring
as the light flashed and played
on snow crystals
ice sheets
insistent river

through the prism of my tears
I laughed   accepted the gift

I tell you
this is a place
for worship

Indelible

"Of recognizing that holiness has its caveat,
the stupidity of self and of humanity among
them."

Brenda Leifso
Excerpt from: Hoo Doos Trail

Margaret Macpherson

It is a big

space

between imaginary lines

marking our mountains
from theirs,

separating our scraggly unshaven spruce
from those beyond

 the thin boundry scars
of transit and time

Big,

like our women
built for birthing and beating

Big this place,

the boreal crosshatch of powerlines and leaseholds

                    the oily after-scent of second day clothes

the distance between
pumpjacks and prostitutes

Margaret Macpherson

the way we keep it together

hold it apart

and guard what is ours

                        through squinted rifle sights

Ian LeTourneau

Pump Jacks

The field was probably a flank of wheat
or flax until the replication of pump jacks
began. In eerie formations,

they infinitely regress into the folds
of prairie, black and red mosquitoes,
practicing their mechanized maneuvers.

In the momentary hesitation of the cog
before the jack's proboscis dips down,
and again down, into the earth,

you imagine the blurred wringing of hands,
the drool of oil from the effortless labour.
Moveable, insatiable, endless.

A.G. Boss

Cutline: a slice of civilization through a forest; a ribbon pierced through timber.

I drive my Chev 3/4 ton 4x4 through ruts on a muddy cutline and at the bottom of a hill there's a bit of a swamp so Pal says, it can't be deep; just go on through, so I say yeah and I giver and we hit the water and it's deep and we jostle and shake forward until we high centre and the tires spin futile and the truck stops dead in wet clay mud.

I sigh. We step out into the sludge and struggle to string out the winch, attach it to a tree, turn it on and the truck is pulled forward inch by inch by inch by inch. We're standing waist-deep in mud and I say to Pal, isn't it something how we fight our way across this earth. Everything is a barrier yet we go everywhere; we won't let anything stop us: if there's a river we build a bridge; if there's an ocean, we construct a boat; if there's a mountain we drill a tunnel; no oxygen, we got tanks; outer space? Here's a rocket. We cut lines through forests to civilize wildness, yet a bit of mud and water traps us and we battle for inches.

Just then a monster Bull Moose slowly strides onto the cutline no more than 50 meters away. I grab my rifle, shoulder it, place the crosshairs gently on his heart and squeeze so softly … and stop. He swings that big head toward us, sniffs the air, and walks across the cutline and into the woods

And Pal says … why didn't you shoot?

A.G. Boss

He was there, I say, in my sights, and then a thought fired into my brain: how are we gonna get off this cutline. And I hesitated and he moved and did you see him? He stepped onto the cutline and vanished into the bush, moving silently through this icy muck as though it was the easiest thing in the world ... and we fight to civilize every inch.

Then I thought: we're on a cutline. A cut line. Get it?

Get what?

A line cut into something alive will bleed until the blood clots and the cut heals. And even if it heals, it becomes a scar. And if it doesn't heal the life slowly seeps out until the being dies.

We are standing on an open wound.

Pal stares at me, for a long long moment. What does that mean, he says? I don't know what it means, I say. I don't know. But I think I'm gonna go home and plant a tree.

Vivian Demuth

Live Earth

The concert goers gather where the earth is slanted
        sheltered from city lights
Where the land still grows verdant words
Not slick pavement and glowing machines
        who fear and suffocate poems
The wandering moon fills their refugee mouths
The homeless wind sprinkles a rouge of cosmic
        dust on their skins to magnetize their memories
An orphaned grizzly cub taps his claw three times
        on a firetower woman's arthritic shoulders
Gray wolves lick Cree words hidden beneath buffalo horns
There are no police with their song and dance
That's for the birds who punctuate the budding
        text from their nests and cover any half-naked chicks
Pine beetles spit three times at the evergreens who cough
        and remind all that the word 'pristine'
        died invisibly in the grey rain long ago
Shadow dinosaurs roar three times then give up their fossils
And as a tired sun rises, it sears the text onto the gathered's
        soiled bodies
The firetower woman feels the marks in the moist forest
        between her toes, three short–three long–three short
Ask her long the game trail and she will reveal the mountain
        text, the understory of the boreal, a rhizomatic SOS

Vivian Demuth

Faders*
for Anna Politkovskaya

What fades?
Evergreens, survivors of chain-linked
generations of logging, now a cemetery
of vertical bones with marrow devoured
by defrosted mobs of mountain beetles.
Dry pine trees, fragile, faded red
like splattered blood of hunted journalists
marked in blinding daylight of corruption
and wars. The paper dollar skin of a million
carved trees changes hands to kill or save
a forest, to pay the salary of a determined
investigative reporter or to complete
the handshake of a prearranged hit.
When the deal is done, baked winds
blow tinder needles into the world's circular
currents where the sad news is read by ever-
globalizing children scavenging through
trashed newspapers. This is the hazardous
graveyard, dumped skeletons of trees and
journalists, the unpredictable resting place
from which a thoughtful spark has potential,
in spite of death, to melt and release
a thousand tender seedlings.

*Forestry term for pine beetle-infested pine tree

Brenda Leifso

Hoo Doos Trail

My mind hiccupping back
to that sweet May smell
of high snowpack melting,
tickling down river beds – glacial shock
to the underbelly of sun-stunned rock –
I keep thinking didn't it smell like rain
to a thirsty traveler, but as usual

there comes the question of honesty. Really
I couldn't have been thinking of travelers,
thirsty or otherwise, for wasn't I lost
in pastoral exultation, the trail
satisfyingly mulchy and under my feet
prairie crocus sproutlings, stalks furred and juicy,
purple buds gearing up for the moment
they'd blow themselves open?
O! to be thus unabashed,
ecclesiastic, but
to admit what was really on my mind:

Rhonda and her red-gorgeous hair
dropping a tick, neat-as-you-please
on her breakfast plate, its arachnoid freeze
as Rhonda herself shrieked a jig around the stunned dining hall –
something about shaving herself bald –
In short, the mercurial nature of the pastoral
when there are creatures to scuttle up the pant leg,
root in our hairy places,
burrow in.

Brenda Leifso

Now, two years later, I would stand on my head
and drink fifty glasses of water to stop spluttering my way
to this trailhead, the strange beginning of
fever and joint aches, the nervous dislocasia
of having lost here some essential thing.
Of recognizing that holiness has its caveats,
the stupidity of self
and of humanity being among them. Which is more ridiculous:
the men on the golf course across the river emerging from
their carts
to brandish their clubs at a grizzly mama and her cubs
or the quick-dry clad, sun-proofed poet standing safe on the far shore,
and with dewy-eyes, watching?
What would I do if mama swam the river –
elocute with affecting verbal line breaks
that I, a concerned and caring steward of the earth,
understood the challenges and perils of her shrinking habitat,
and therefore should not be eaten?

Mama bear, you can
pry off its legs, cut it in half,
flail its carapace with a hammer,
but a tick in danger will blindly tunnel deeper.

Carol MacKay

Saturday, Waiting Outside the Recording Studio Barn
Ryley, Alberta

The trees lay a backing track against a lead shot sky;
just a slight buzzing, like breath blown through the teeth of a comb
and the periodic cracking of puddle ice.
There are mole songs, humming, running beneath the receding snow,
this year unnerving. Quieter.
The fire in our exhaust speeds the lazy thaw,
forces new hiding places as it radiates a half circle from the pipe.

This place knows it will be gone. Maybe not next year but soon.
It is the consequence of engaging in creative audacity
above veins of coal: 312 square kilometres of compressed darkness.
When the skin of this land turns inside out to expose ancient bones,
folksongs of the living, its gyroscope will bend, stop the spin because
land doesn't bargain.
It knows current for beard trimmers, rotating tie racks, rice cookers
is the only currency.
Worry-free over the dumping of oxides,
green-sounding particulates
that seep deep into its music,
it simply plays the notes given.

Our Imprint on the Land

"Sometimes
when they are open
the horizon and the eye slit
will see and speak
as one."

Weyman Chan
Excerpt from: Near Milk River,
looking for the Sweetgrass Hills

Marion Brooker

Seasons

I run barefoot in spring
not because of need but because of desire
splash in roadside puddles, feel mud ooze up through toes
Feet feeling winter retreat deep
into the earth, hiding, regrouping.
My feet drum the mating call of spring.

I run barefoot in summer
run barefoot until calluses no longer wince at each stone, skirt each thistle
run feeling warmth of freshly turned garden soil, rooting worms with toes
burrowing deep until tiny tendrils of new forming carrots curl around.
When Sun scorches Earth's moistness I run cool rhubarb patches seeking shady Solace.
Run pastures where rustling grass signals snakes and cows chew cuds, where bees barter
nectar for pollen with bluebells and buttercups, vetch and cowslips

I run barefoot in fall
when stubbled fields sharpened by cooling nights stab at my soles
soles callused to their barb
run in woods high with cranberries signaling pregnancy
run, tilted skyward, to beating rhythms of geese departures
Leaves, narcisstic in their vibrancy, shiver reluctance to fall to decay
I crunch and squish in their dying

I read the seasons with my feet
My feet shuffle the dance of winter
Manacled muffled
no longer sensitive to changing earth
a tentative soft shoe dance
on land waxed slick with ice and snow
They wait
wait until snow slushes
wait until sap rises reluctantly
 stamp their impatience
for trees and buds and hope to preen
for spring.

Feet free of manacles leave

footsteps in the land

Vivian Hansen

Touching Trees

And he says he shivered
when I showed him the picture of the poplars hugging
what are the chances
of finding two poplars entwined
for all their tree eternity?

or finding their fossilized coupling
amongst hundreds that grow
in a straight and narrow stretch
to dry prairie sky

I seek the greeting
of inaudible-to-human
dryad moans
I hope to hear, as my own voice
curves around you/with you
and people will say: they just grew together
      just like that.

he remembered holding their young suckers together
forced them into Siamese growth, just because he could.
forgot them for fifty years
until I found them in the forest
on the margins of the old homestead.

Richard Stevenson

Pete's Dilemma
for Peter Polet

Do I cut 'er down
for a view of the mountain
and star-strewn lake

or do I wait until
we're a pair of bad teeth
that need to be removed?

I'm thinking it'd be a shame,
but the view from the sundeck
would be vastly improved –

It's just – well, holding the train
of her sumptuous green gown, just now
bumptiously flouncing up the path,

this cedar could be my daughter,
teetering on high heels,
out of breath, a little tipsy ... .

What is she so anxious to say?
Why is she so out of breath?
Why must the wind cry Mary?

Weyman Chan

Near Milk River, looking for the Sweetgrass Hills

I did not come here
to excuse my self
or anyone else. It was
because the feathered bracts
and wind whipped stalks that
dry-lashed the warbler and her cheek

slant morning brow
like a forgiving aunt
wearing her hat shadow in this remarkable
early heat, which seemed to sigh

for more leafhoppers braying, "rotten wood can't be carved"—
that I felt the dryness of the grass.
The dewless brown quench of hard ground.

Dryness,
regret turned whole. Thrush
scold on willow stump
flared for some shorewards
ash or elder berry to
raise its small body
like seed
before high summer dried them
behind an autumn cloud

browner than the gospel vegetation in this desert
I thought to myself: is it stoopless
distance that breeds the next vee
migrating beads and needles of moisture,

Weyman Chan

black nibble
of the fly,
the black lick of deer scat turned
home, as the deer make their way in single file across Milk River?

Last year I saw them. Today they were
as empty as that warbler was,
behind her veil of grass.

Every sound and tree is a hermit.
Not every hermit is a sound or tree.
Sometimes the quiet act of following
your own past will address the future. And will be

given back as it began.
Sometimes
when they are open,
the horizon and the eye slit
will see and speak
as one.

Diane Buchanan

October

There's loneliness here today.
Tall stems of sedge chafe on unpredictable
breezes. A month ago the bulrushes
held dark heads high above the grasses, now
they are grey and moulting. Scent of tickle,
mildew and musk ride the surly air.
No green here, only a dry, wizened brown
beneath a sky feathered in clouds, the sun
struggling to warm the earth –
to warm me.

The one with the crooked wing
was the last to leave. Took more time
to learn how to fly. Now she has her own nest,
doesn't come back anymore. Left us behind
to feed her rabbits, her dog, her horse, try to find uses
for four empty bedrooms that echo
girlish laughter, teen angst, Garth Brooks–
a silent phone.

One pair of mallards still bob in the center
of the riffling gun metal surface. For this water
there is no leaving, no coming, only staying,
the accepting of more, the possibility of less. Retreat
has already begun. Maps of algae are left
burping alkaline bubbles in the shrunken muddy
edges no longer able to conceal the human humilities,
empty pop cans, beer bottles, cigarette packages,
MacDonald's coffee cups. Hard to hide flaws
when you're left behind and everything around
is withering. This place, this island of water

Diane Buchanan

in a sea of prairie, once so alive, so vital,
so necessary, is now abandoned and superfluous.

A yellow butterfly rises up
out of the rushes, sparks my shadow,
flickers south. I follow.

Jenna Butler

winter highway

November   we descend
from permafrost north
camp on the ice

fire on a bier
above the river
poplar logs   green and sappy
snow pitted from
the flankers' fall

all day   we follow
the trucks gone before
    chancing rotten ice
    for tea   white bread
    ten-pound sacks of potatoes

fifty kilometres upriver
men detox on the trap lines
wait   for the trucks to return
for their friends to come through
with rum   with whiskey

all summer
the settlement has sunk into itself
feral   bald-toothed

has squatted by the river
squinted blearily into
the hazy sunshine

waited for the ice

Tom Wayman

Not Every Highway Has a Number

Steering the lazy S-curves
that descend to meander beside a creek
then angle up the walls of a ravine
onto undulating flatland again
and a view of ranges
blue and icy with the distant cold

      Or in blown snow
      that crosses the pavement in waves
      higher than my vehicle, the gusts
      increasing in force and duration
      until I enter a whiteout
      of buffeting flakes: only the hood visible
      ahead, and a white line on asphalt to my right
      intermittently glimpsed
      in the storm's brief lulls
      Geared down to low, tensed for
      a wreck splayed across the blizzard
      or someone overtaking me who misjudges
      the friction possible on this frozen surface
      I inch onward, the cabin around me
      with its ordinary seats, pile of CDs,
      more real that the bright blankness
      streaming past every window
      Then the shock of
      a blurred figure in the centre of the road
      gesturing at me
      with the bulk of a jackknifed tractor-trailer behind
      slammed into a pickup, another shadow
      signaling me to crawl past
      groups of men, a row of cars
      stopped beyond the catastrophe

Tom Wayman

Or the freeway that cleaves to a valley bottom
until the route lifts higher inland to avoid a bluff
before dropping again to scud on by a wide river
Engine and wheels and blacktop
rolling smooth as sky, as flame
as a quick-tempo, mellifluous folk tune about
a wanderer's love of
both city blocks and open country

      The two-lanes and four-lanes we accelerate down
      are not only artificial constructs
      but breathe through our encounters with them
      —each highway a colossal sculpture
      whose shapes and textures our tires, our presence
      touch and respond to
      just how a symphonic work
      takes form via notation, rehearsals and an eventual cascade of
      phrasing, key changes, inflections, pauses
      that exist in the ear, the mind
      —engineering of culverts and surface
      leveling, compacting, the requisite
      bank to curves, all
      performed, traveled, that carry us
      across stretches of time and distance
      —every road with its own essence: signatures, bars, movements where
      our thoughts drift, and other passages
      that rear up foremost in our being: where we live
      in this music, this art, this
      transport that out of so much labor and
      chord progressions, infelicities and solutions
      reaches from the past to offer
      a crafted, communal
      munificence

Brenda Leifso

Driving the 22

Driving the 22 north, noon sun and wind
warm on the arm in the ears
through the rolled down window
kd lang's Hymns rolling too
through the long-grassed foothills
and you beside me,
the baby snoozing in the back seat,
it's so hard not to feel drowsily,
contentedly alive, river water and campground dust
in the nooks of my elbows, my toes,
on my fingers and the gearshift the sticky sweet reminder
of Okanagan peaches and cherries, like our little red car
summer has stuffed us to the gills.

My eyelids too lazy, want sleep.
I pull off so you can steer us home
both of us believing
we've sifted out disaster, the last miles
like sugar through our fingers,
but the deer's out of the ditch so fast
she's memory before I see her
dekes once, twice,
slams across the hood, twists
the car to a stop. A moment to figure out
the glass in my lap isn't windshield,
you're body isn't wrapped around the steering wheel,
and the baby is squalling angry only to have been woken
so abruptly. Deer on the road beside us, heaving.

Later, we'll make a joke out of it–
worse for the deer –

Brenda Leifso

but we both know there's nothing funny about her
inability to stand, how she sideways heaves herself into the ditch.
Nothing funny about the camping axe you fish from the trunk,
hold for a long time in your hand,
me nursing the baby on the roadside,
pretending not to watch.
What then is there to do but drive home?
Clumps of bloody hair sticking to the hood,
but no one and nothing else holding us
to account, our blind-sided empathy
criminal, the highway and the wind rolling home
without ceremony.

Pierrette Requier

Sketches of a Return, February 2006

We leave the dusty city in a grey that is
more dull than boring, a drought grey
that returns me to my worst fears—
that nothing ever changes,
is as dreadful as *they* said *it* was—
like a bad hangover I try to sleep off as
the wind picks up, rocks the truck.

In half sleep, a yearning for home, for what
is known in the bones, gnaws—as visceral as the smell
of mom's baked bread—for the soothing and familiar.
Is this familiarity something we make up or reinvent
for comfort? To heal a homesickness
rooted way, way back to the unsettling settling
of this vast land, this Last Great West?

The return comes slowly, and on the land's terms:
in lit-up spruce tops, the dance of snow-lined branches,
tire tracks on side roads, in aspen birch poplars'
straight glossy trunks the colour of *mon petit Missel* cover,
in the blue-black puddled highway,
in willow bark's finishing touches—
that old-fashioned, serious red—
a sharp balm in this wintry country.

At the Smoky River, the old jolt of abrupt fear,
of shift in landscape–
the danger of curve, of hill, of down and up,
the narrow bridge–giving in to
a vast terror we try to hide, contain,
in our flat, furrowed, snow-lined fields,

Pierrette Requier

our wire-fenced quarter sections,
in power lines running along the highway.

The return opens its arms at sunset
in a water colour wash of   blue   under wash of
pink   spilling into a sky full of   mauve,
in the slowness of the sun's long arc sinking
and what goes on under pond
surfaces   hinting at the coming of spring,
at long summer nights.

There is something, always too big here.
A long low cloud breaks the dread of flatness,
open to all of heaven.
Ponds hold pieces of sky.
The horizon will not give comfort.
Snow pulls the prairie open even more
spreads it out *à perte de vue*
Thin trees write this space.

The Land's Imprint on Us

"The dust of this land
of wind and blue sky
forms a burr under my skin ."

Rob K. Omura
Excerpt from:
Great Lone Land

Kathy Fisher

this landscape

how may i melt into this landscape   this flat flat land   the gas flares
dotting the grass tabletop   like kids' birthday candles   one here   one there   spotty and
fuming   the crunchy crabgrass   three mows a season   the dusty earth

this is not my home yet i stretch for the sky uncaps me   my head heart floats up   flies
up free from all its Eastern shoulds and dos   here there is today   now   though that
changes quickly   or not at all   the point is: be prepared for everything   for all kinds
of weather   in any season   snow or sleet or singeing hot scorchers   even when it's wet
it's dry   the earth pushes away the water so it sits on the surface pooled   like mercury
escaped from a thermometer   until the clay grabs it   until it is driven down by tractor
tires   churning and blending   gumbo   the kind of muck you can't stop in   like
quicksand   keeps you on the move on the hoof

alkaline leeches mark empty sloughs   cracked and crater-like   no water in these tracks
these holes   these birthday basins   no newborn baby-smooth skin   just crowsfeet and
crone's wrinkles   like mummified apples   all ancient   the sweetness puckered out

i swim in this dryness   dive into this dust   skinny dip in sage and spear grass
springboard up   into this sky borne sea

Deborah Lawson

Dominion of Wind

Wind …
your voice keening across the prairie
comes to me in foreign languages,
a whisper in the aspen thicket,
or heavily accented with evergreen,
your breath smelling of spruce gum
and camphor.

At first
I did not like you, did not trust
your movements as you stirred, or the clanging
as you rattled the bars of the branched cages
where you lived and moved in your malign being.
I feared the dirges I heard at night,
moaning all the parts of a dead day's requiem,
spilling lamentation into the unfriendly darkness.
Even the owl, so wise and silent,
fled your mournful urgency, swooping
low and shadowy, moonlight-chased, across
the open spaces of our yard.

No matter where I went, you followed, shook free
of every bowery prison, made fugitive haste to stay
proximate, arcing high over tumbled terrain,
skimming the plateau of flat country. Stalking me.

Or so I thought.
And yet—in this expansive, lonely land
you changed your speech, put threats away, rippled
through ripening fields, beguiled me

Deborah Lawson

with a resonant song, an undertone
of symphonic excitement felt in my veins.

How could I not respond?
I open to you, take you deep within,
become breath of your breath

Rob K. Omura

Great Lone Land

A hot iron sun blazes
sometimes the colour of wild roses,
and at others, golden rod and flax,
and brands the tips of an endless sky.

The wind never stops here.

The wind, it blows east,
riding long freight trains
to a point beyond the parallax
of Kreisel's broken globe.

Thunderheads lick a flat earth
with wet kisses and rainbow promises
of mythical gold
to be found
at the edge of the Canadian Shield.

This land, this Great Lone Land,
humbles me, always will,
and makes me so unbearably small.

The dust of this land
of wind and blue sky
forms a burr under my skin
sea spray can never wash out
even after years.

Awash in waist high grass
at the crest of a bluff,
I tack into the wind
to return to my car.

Rob K. Omura

Mitchell once heard
the wind whisper his name
in the coulees
where cottonwood and sagebrush
cling to creek banks
and Palliser watered his horses.

If you listen closely,
you can still hear voices
in the rumble of tires
against tar highways
where traffic streams
on a hot summer's day.

Rob K. Omura

At the Frank Slide Interpretative Centre

The highway through the graveyard
of Frank is a granite moonscape
that glows bone white at night.
But we drove through in August heat
that melted the waxy wings of angels,
the sun bearing down to warm the dead.
Even flies curl up under stones.

Here, the blue turtle's ancient sleep broke.
A single fin drooped down to shatter dreams.
Humble Frank is silent now, still, lulled
to sleep by the weight of lullabies.
Limestone clouds clutter the streets where
the walking mountain lumbered to a stop.

Today the turtle, she sleeps again.
She dreams the valley back into being.
Sometimes she snores and chases silver trout upstream
but never catches them.

Across the valley a caravan of buses
beetles up a paved road, coughing
tourists in the dusty parking lot.
A Babel of languages tumbles out
welcomes the day.
Cameras stamp postcard smiles,
silver oxide fixed to digital paper
licked and posted, dropped in a box.

From the gift shop window
next to empty t-shirts swelling with hope,

Weyman Chan

a dreamcatcher
casts a net over the mountain,
but she always slips through the mesh.

One day she'll hear her name called
awaken, yawn
forget her dreams
and with one stony sneeze –
the valley will cease to exist.

Barbara Janusz

on the brink of the slide

panorama of jagged boulders confronts me, jars me into denial
I don't fathom that I'm passing through a graveyard
nor grieve the shattered bodies of whole families,
uprooted homes entombed by a landslide of limestone.

like an affliction, the mountain hovers incessantly over my shoulder
when I walk I can't help but stare
as when a disfigured person boards a bus or train
cements the gaze of passengers
Turtle Mountain, a century ago, within span of a hundred seconds
- in geological time, a cleft second
defied its immutability, lost its face
its collapse fomented a gigantic scar
obscured by advent of the darkest season
cloud blankets its wound in snow
disperses, reveals its camouflaged predictability.

when Mars orbited so close
its crimson circumference so strikingly dissimilar from other celestial bodies
the pale luminescence of a crescent moon starkly silhouetted your nakedness
and made a mockery of my reverence for your permanence.

Anna Mioduchowska

Blowing at the Sky

Dreaming across the face of a snow-tipped mountain,
one Golden Eagle.

It's just before sunset,
but voices urging south muffle hunger, fatigue,
the bird will not sleep tonight.
Three hundred solitary shadows
cast over the limestone since morning,
each one a kingdom unto itself.

An old man by the river,
open ledger, telescope.
Two women taking turns with children,
binoculars, a sixteen-year old
speaking in tongues:

over number 3,
        left of Mt. Rundle,
                approaching big smile,
each pair of eyes glued to a spec of dust,
the count must be accurate,
                leaving the second cliff
        over the big hole.

It's a young one,
the river whispers in a gravelly voice.

To the east, giants cross swords
over who will pluck the last lobster from the sea,
to the west, they butt heads
for the last fir fit for lumber.

Anna Mioduchowska

On the grassy shore of the Kananaskis,
an old man adds a checkmark in the appropriate space,
two women massage their necks,
a boy breathes in breathes out.

Sliding from one updraft to the next,
the eagle.

Ben Murray

Finders Keepers

under slate Drumheller skies
we seek the past–
not the outsized pomp and glory
of dino bone, just
ancient oysters, hidden fossil
beds we long to un-tuck, to un-sheet

it is late afternoon, the sun
a rumour now, badland winds
our chorus; our guidebook
as vague as the sky,
your hopeful smile
guide enough for me

rock-hug succulents and cacti
drink the air as we pass, and I thirst
for a kiss, hugging the flesh
on your bones, our tongues explore,
finders keepers

minutes later you spot our first
find of the new century–
on a scree-filled hill aspiring to cliff
you've kicked up oyster traces,
your gleeful shouts a songline
in this winded world

packs soon bulging with oyster plunder
we consummate this Ordovician afternoon

Ben Murray

doffing our many layers
we make love on the rocks,
on these oyster beds,
the blush-red bloom of Ball Cacti
prickly voyeurs to the action,
our sweat and wet a memory
tease of sea-swallowing days

Kerry Mulholland

Drumheller

the desert makes me lonely but not in a thirsty way
pictures of earth from space are lonely
round blue skinned so thin with cloud and air
water echoes here in the gully and undulation
even lizard flows
a small river over sand
great seas have been and gone
hear the quiet receding
the slow revelation of dry
the way skin and flesh fall away
until the glistening bone is known

Born from the Land

"Yes, that's what I remember best."

Rosemary Griebel
Excerpt from:
Clam Digging in the Battle River

Marion Brooker

An Anthem

I will thunder the drum of stampeding buffalo. I will cry with the crashing
scorched bones in the sun

I will ride the train whistle over ripe prairie grain fields, over land yet untouched
by the
hand on the plow
I will raise my glass to monuments of loneliness of sacrifice of hopes
to   broken promises of barren rainclouds

I will fade in the distance a wisp of a whisper then ricochet back through dark
mountain passes
I will tell of the people who rode that train whistle with visions and with plans
and with fear
in their bellies
of voices that blended but kept their own cadence
I will honour the people who drove the steel forward their gift to a country yet
unshaped or one

I will smell in the burning of flesh during branding
I will hear in the gush of oil released
the secrets of cowhands
the secrets of roughnecks, couched
in words of their trade
a language their own

I will honour the women who fought to be people

I will gasp the first breath of next generations
I will sway to the music of songs
yet unsung
I will wail on the wind of times left behind. I will write on the stones of times
still to come
dip my paddle in founts of swift flowing rivers
Baptize in the name of snow rain and sun

the people
the land

Gayle Sacuta

Vast Prairie Puja

Uncle leads
past antiquated
threshers.
I trail behind, step-in-step,
wind baths my face
sparrows whistling,
to the farthest, littlest evergreen
shelter-belt pivot.
Pulls grass,
gives attention,
says nothing.
Our offer complete, we turn
back from the vulnerable
edge of the farm,
where it drops off
into the vast prairie sky

Gayle Sacuta

Where Are You From?

I'm from
Byemoor - no - that's a town.
From a farm, near
Gough Lake.
Okay. An alkaline
slough bottom.
How much land?
Seems like
a big number
but everything's relative,
even home.
I come from as much land as a man can farm
singularly with occasional help
in busy seasons.

Carol MacKay

Scandinavian Picnic at Markerville

The idle burnish of an ancient cowbell grows courage on a barn nail.
The sun, bright as an Icelandic night,
sends a satisfied gleam across the buckboard-wide table
crowded by near empty silver-capped jars: Gran's jaw-shrinking dills
and vegetable marrow, prunes in sweet profusion, placed around bowls
empty of slaw and chicken.

We set out, refreshed warriors, into the bush
where cocklebur wounds, nettle gangrene fells us,
one by one into a respectable death, worthy of Valhalla.

Resurrected by the evening's cool peace
we sing in the hayfield, sharing space with the giants of Jötunheim.
This impossible mixing of realms, of dwarf and elf,
possible only under a seafaring sky.

Jenna Butler

Farmhouse, Castor

early sun limns
the plate rail   a kitchen
reduced to grit & shambles
     butcher block table
     wallpaper slumped about its knees

light here reveals
only   absence

teasel in the bones of
the victory garden   thrusting
barrel staves like iron ribs

what we have come for

lilacs pressing in
these diamond panes   their blossom
stark & fragrant across the hearth
     rainwater shifting in
     the stair's curved spine

how this land holds everything &
nothing   back

Rosemary Griebel

Clam Digging in the Battle River

That summer wild raspberries flamed
on the banks of the Battle River
as we blinded through murky waters
searching for clams. The air smelled of eternity,
the summer promised a life bigger than a town.
Filling a bucket with dark rocks of shell
we conjured the palpable curve of the future:
you would pilot a plane so high
above the land the moon would be
your sole companion, and I would go west,
skip words over the shifting light of water.
When you touched my hair I could not look at you
or the hungry mouth of sky. We gathered
buck brush and dried grass for the fire
as a hymn of hornets hung above us.
The clams danced over white flames
until their reluctant shells surrendered.
Inside they were all muck and disappointment.
I gave the shells back to the sweep of water
as you called to me from the other shore.
The air that summer, full and sweet.
Yes, that's what I remember best.
Only the ancient river doesn't question the way.

Susan Picard

Power of the Land

Last time I was home I borrowed your boots and took a stroll
Past the spring down to the river where I watched the waters roll
Then it was back up the hill, across the field and past the stock
I savoured all the sights and sounds and smells while on my walk…

And remembering now it's funny how I feel
It's like this my other life just isn't real
And the smell of manure could bring me back
To that old familiar beaten track
Where I'd go to get the cows
How I wish I were there now.

I swore when I left, I'd never be a farmer's wife
I saw how hard you worked Mom and I didn't want that life
It was up early milking cows, up late keeping supper warm
With Dad out in the fields it was like you'd both married the farm

And remembering now it's funny how I feel
It's like this my other life just isn't real
And I remember the times to be had
On the tractor next to Dad
Pulling the old plow
How I wish I were there now.

I think now's the time, I can't believe that I've lived to see this day
Where I'd toss out all my paperwork just to go and pile hay And I don't
know how it happened, I think I've come to understand
Just what you always told me about the power of the land…

Carol MacKay

Selling the Family Farm

The hole in my father's field.
appeared overnight in the fallow field
where the sign post entered hard-packed ground.
From the highway side of the fence I see
weathervane falling, disoriented, all wind
into the widening gap.

Not one word.
The trailer tips over onto its shortest side,
funnelled into a sooty end.
Not one word so I could try.

This is entirely my fault line.
I will revisit this place in muttering dreams
black sheep unaware of black ink setting on paper:
the last pitched bale stamped "vendor's copy"
The green I knew will be gasified into portable, unpotable green.
This queasy ground hides more than bones and septic tanks
And its not just coal and syn-gas stock
coming up.

Cheryl King

Grandpa Moves the Hay

'hey, bud!
got the tractor running
let's put a bale in the feeder
for Cres & the Bob!'

lightly and lovingly
she invites him out of the recliner
into coveralls & a mild January morning

tugging a cap
low over his ears
he grips the handrail
descends the porch carefully
one step at a time

leaning on her arm
he climbs into the half ton
and we head back
to the big shed
for the tractor

pulling himself into the tractor cab
labours the old heart & he pauses
breathing hard
settles, adjusts, readies

gravel crunches
and the tractor lumbers
through the dim shed
prowling towards the bale stack
like a hungry, slow-moving agri-beast

Cheryl King

sharp tines pierce a fat round bale
& the journey begins

slowly
he guides the tractor & the bale
to the corral
outside the gate
he sets the bale down
maneuvers
to grab the bale on end

she opens the gate
shoos the horse & calf aside
stands beside the big circle
of welded pipe

arms raised
she signals by hand

he watches each gesture
adjusts hydraulic levers
shifting half a ton of hay
as easily as you or I handle
a salad fork

now!
her arms drop

he releases the grapple
the rich green round of hay
settles into the metal crib
perfectly centered &
dropped in place

Cheryl King

a lifetime of farming
to move the hay
today

Steven Michael Berzensky

The Last Days of Mrs. Allen

for Brian Wilson and family in Red Deer

I was born in Montana
before we came here to Alberta.
Oh, how I wish I had those old days again.

* * *

I use to have a lot of photographs of us.
But my family got away with them.
Divided them.

We had some that were framed.
Photographs of the horses
and us girls on them, racing.

One horse we brought up from a colt.
And all we had to do is whistle
and she'd come.

She would always come running
and lay her head on our shoulders.
She'd take her nose and rub us.

* * *

Oh, I will never forget when we lost our dad.
He use to raise his own horses.
Oh, I was quite an age when he died.

132

Steven Michael Berzensky

I was the oldest of the three of us.
All girls.
No brothers.

We had cousins, though,
who use to stay with us,
and they were good.

My sister, the one closest to me,
was quite a rider, too.
We use to ride at the fairs.

Father taught us.
He was a great horseman.
When he died,

I missed him and missed him.
I still miss him.
He was a big man.

* * *

Animals. They're the ones who know.
We use to ride them at the fair.
Win our races.   Never use a whip.
That was cruel. Just stroke them.

My father was a great horseman.
They use to call him the Old Man and his girls.
That's what they use to call us.
We didn't care.

Steven Michael Berzensky

Our horses, they wouldn't let any stranger on them.
They'd just hump their backs and pitch them off.
Horses know. They're not given credit.
But a horse does know.

I've never seen horses like the ones we raised.
They'd be out in the field and Father'd just whistle.
And they didn't walk to him, they'd run.
And lay their head on his shoulder.

* * *

When old Bessie died,
Father made a coffin for her.
She was about nine years old.

She had the best of care, too.
Just like a person.
She was little.

Didn't weigh much more than a colt.
Oh, old Bessie, she'd come
no matter where she was.

And she would always come running
and lay her head on our shoulder.
Oh, I miss them. I miss them all.

Andy Michaelson

Grandfathers

I knew
no grandfathers
gone, before my creation
Piegan, Blood, Siksika, Tsuu T'ina, Haida, Gitksan, Dene
speak often of their grandfathers
pride and respect
in their words

I imagine theirs
are mine
seeking wisdom
discovering patience
by listening, watching

The grandfathers teach
learn to fly from the hawk
soar high, clear eyed
learn to sing from the meadowlark
sweet, in perfect pitch
learn to speak from the eagle
without enmity, after due consideration
learn to think from the owl
without distractions, considering all
learn to move from the fox
quiet, without disturbing the landscape

Learn to swim from the salmon
nourish many, returning to renew
learn to live from the lodge pole pine
straight, offering shelter to all
learn to laugh from the brook

Andy Michaelson

swift, joining others to be the river
learn to protect from the bear
leave your print sometimes
so all will know who guards
the earth mother

Learn to be wary of man
remembering
that which they don't understand
they destroy

See a horizon
listen to your land

Make your bed
in a hidden place
keep it secret
go there each day
breathe a wind

Bob Stallworthy

Connect the Dots

the sky is so big in this place
it can fill the space between father and son

the land is a firmament under it
highways in straight lines
connect dots
stars on the landscape

we come from a place
where the lines on the land are not straight
where the map doesn't always tell us
how to get there and the sky is much smaller

where there are too many things for it to run into
the edge of the ocean forests of black spruce
places where it and the road twisting
simply disappear from view

here we are stars within stars
it would be so easy for us to let that old space
that twists and turns across our landscapes
fill black as asphalt

 instead we use the sky and straight lines
to keep from getting lost

Afterword

Putting Writing in its Place

Tom Wayman

I believe, as the U.S. poet/philosopher Wendell Berry has argued, that all knowledge is rooted in a place. So in order for anyone to understand what he or she thinks they know, they need to be aware of the place in which she or he lives, the urban or rural locale in which that knowledge is situated. Where does this place's water come from, and via what means does it arrive here? Electrical power? Food? Why is there such economic, educational, environmental and other quality-of-life disparity among the people who inhabit this place, and how does this disparity threaten or enhance his or her own existence? What, therefore, needs to be done to decrease--or increase, if that is your goal--this disparity?

Because I am convinced that knowledge is about a *place*, to me every writer "writes the land", whether by omission or commission. By what a writer doesn't say, doesn't pay attention to, the rest of us can hear in the silences the writer's attitude toward the world that the writer inhabits.

We exist in a time of enormous obfuscation about the realities of existence, a purposeful confusion generated on behalf of corporations and governments with a vested interest in having people turn away from understanding their own daily lives and instead to project their natural curiosity about the world toward the lives of social parasites mostly resident elsewhere--entertainers, vacuous "celebrities", sports stars, politicians. I daresay more Albertans know the name of Paris Hilton's former pet dog than know the names of those tribes in Afghanistan whose men, women and children are being blown apart by NATO forces on behalf of a corrupt narco-administration propped up by foreign troops and a consortium of native warlords. Never has it been more important for Canadian writers to speak clearly, effectively, about the place in which we live and the details of the lives we and our fellow citizens are able to construct in this locale.

This task for authors has never been more difficult, in that never has the population been so relentlessly encouraged to escape into corporate- and technologically-mediated illusions. "All human economy is still land-based," Berry warns, in a speech at a 2005 globalization conference. "To the extent that we must eat and drink and be clothed, sheltered and warmed, we live from the land. The idea that we have now progressed from a land-based economy to an economy based on information is a fantasy." The U.S. poet Gary Snyder states in his essay "Tawny Grammar" (1990), that we are immersed in "the delusion that we are each a kind of 'solitary knower'--that we exist as rootless intelligences without layers of localized contexts." Snyder points out that the place in which we live, including the landscape, people, tools, myths, stories, and biosphere that surround us, "is what we *think with* [his emphasis]." The concept that somehow we need no longer pay attention to where we live, that we in the Canadian West are *Post-Prairie,* as the unfortunate title of one recent literary anthology has it, is not only entirely absurd, but plays completely into the hands of those who seek to enrich themselves by means of our distraction from paying attention to where we are and what is happening to us here.

Our species is capable of insight and self-delusion, of altruism and selfishness, of generosity and greed, of fellow-feeling and solipsism. Every artist needs to think hard about to what ends their art is dedicated. When we through our art understand, love and defend the land in which we dwell, we have a chance to contribute to blunting if not defeating the designs the powers of hate and fear and avarice have on our own lives and the lives of our communities. "With no surroundings there can be no path," Snyder stresses in his essay, "and with no path one cannot become free."

Contributors

John Bishop Ballem is a Calgary novelist, poet and lawyer. He has published 12 novels, a volume of poetry and a textbook on oil and gas law. Many of his poems have appeared in literary journals and magazines.

Steven Michael Berzensky (aka Mick Burrs) is a prize-winning author (*Variations on the Birth of Jacob*, 1997). The first of his many poetry books and chapbooks was published in Alberta in 1971. While residing in Edmonton (1969-1973), he became a freelance producer at CKUA Radio with his series Stand Tall on the Rubble Pile. Mick also performed his own songs in local coffeehouses. He is a former editor of the literary magazine *Grain* (1988-1990) and founder of the Annual Short Grain Contest. After residing in Saskatchewan for 32 years, he moved to Toronto in 2005.

A.G. (Allan) Boss is the Entertainment & Drama Producer for CBC Radio in Alberta. For the CBC he recently produced *Five Hole: Hockey Erotica* with *One Yellow Rabbit Theatre* and *The Rheostatics*. He also recently produced and directed the radioplays *An Eye For An Eye* by Ghost River Theatre and *Conversations with my Neighbour's Pitbull* by Clem Martini for CBC's *Sunday Showcase*. *An Eye For An Eye* has been honoured by being chosen to appear in the world festival of radiodrama, *Worldplay 2007*. Boss's CBC Ideas program *updrafts* – a docudrama about recovering from a brain injury – was nominated for a 2004 *Peabody Award*, a *New York Festivals Award*, a *Gabriel Award* and a *Prix Italia*.

Marion Brooker wrote for youth for many years through Educational Radio. In her recent book for young readers, *Noreen and The Amazing No-Good Horse*, Marion enjoyed reliving experiences of her childhood growing up on a farm in southern Manitoba. At present she is working on a creative non-fiction book based on letters home from her 17 year old uncle who was killed at the Battle of the Somme in 1916. Marion lives in Edmonton with her husband, happily surrounded by family, grandchildren and their pets.

Diane Buchanan is a poet and essayist who learned to love the land during the last thirty-six years living on a farm on the outskirts of Edmonton. She recently moved into the city and is now missing the northern sky, sunsets, night sounds as well as her daily walks to the slough near her home. She is the author of two book of poetry; *Ask Her Anything*, Rowen Books, 2001 and *Between the Silences*, Frontenac House, 2005.

Jenna Butler is an educator, book reviewer, editor and poet. Her work has won a number of awards and has been widely published in literary magazines, journals and anthologies in North America and Europe. She has edited nineteen collections of poetry in Canada and England, and is currently working toward a PhD in Creative and Critical Writing from the University of East Anglia, UK. Her new collection of poems, *Forcing Bloom*, is scheduled for release by Mercutio Press in 2007. Butler lives in Edmonton, Alberta with her husband, where she is the founding editor of Rubicon Press.

Weyman Chan, who works and lives in Calgary, is author of one book of poetry, *Before A Blue Sky Moon* (Frontenac House, 2002). His next book of poems, *Noise From the Laundry* (Talonbooks, 2008) will be released this coming spring. He's currently working on both his third and fourth books of poetry, tentatively entitled, *rain doubt* and *Hypo-derm*.

Marlene Dean has lived in Alberta since 1970. A teacher, she has taught both in the public school system and at the University of Lethbridge. Her writing has appeared in publications such as the ATA newsletter and *The Lethbridge Herald*. Her poem, "Picasso Divorce," was included in *Tesseracts 5*, edited by Robert Runte and Yves Meynard.

Vivian Demuth is the author of a poetry collection, *Breathing Nose Mountain* (Long Shot Productions), and an ecological novel, *Eyes of the Forest* (Smoky Peace Press). Each summer, she hosts an annual eco-poetry event at Nose Mountain in the boreal forest.

Kathy Fisher practices poetry out loud. Her collaboration with the Raving Poets Band sparked the production of her first spoken word CD, *think of me naked*, in 2001. Her voice has been heard on CBC, CJSR and CKUA. In 2002, she appeared nationwide on CBC's alternative arts program, ZeD TV, in its inaugural week.

Myrna Garanis's Edmonton front window looks out on lawns and magpies, not mountains; still, the Rockies tempt and torment. Myrna's poems appear in recent issues of *CV2* and *Room of One's Own*. She is currently involved in *Eyeing the Magpie*, a performance/writing project in collaboration with four other poets.

Rosemary Griebel's poems have been published in a variety of media including literary magazines, CBC Radio, on buses, anthologies and in a chapbook edited by Patrick Lane. She attributes her appreciation of light, space and language to growing up on the Canadian prairie.

Vivian Hansen recently won *Legacy Magazine's* first annual poetry contest. Her poetry, essays and non-fiction have been published in several journals and anthologies, including *Our*

Grandmothers, Ourselves and *Threshold*. Her poetry collection *Leylines of My Flesh* chronicles the experiences of Danish immigrants to western Canada. Her chapbook, "Angel Alley," voices the victims of Jack the Ripper. Vivian has also been active in the Calgary Spoken Word Festival.

A graduate from the University of Alberta with Bachelors of Arts and Laws degrees, **Barbara Janusz** resides in the Crowsnest Pass, where she is engaged as a contributing writer for *EnviroLine, The Business Publication for the Environmental Industry*. Runner up winner of the Jon Whyte Memorial Essay Prize in 2001, she has published essays, short stories and poetry in various literary journals, anthologies and magazines.

Wendy Joy is a member of the Edmonton Stroll of Poets and also often performs with the Raving Poets. She is published in *Freefall*, *The Prairie Journal*, and on the Raving Poets CD I Love Alberta Beat. Her poem "Hot Sheets, Really" won 3rd prize in *Freefall's* 2006 writing contest.

The oldest in a farm family and raised near the Battle River at Wainwright, **Cheryl King** is familiar with canola fields, rolling hills, beaver dams, cow pastures, poplar trees, the smell of grain dust and the bawling of calves in late fall. For the past 16 years she has lived in Grande Prairie. A busy consultant & educator, she works too much, reads endlessly, wishes for more time to play with paper & paint, and is occasionally blessed by having a poem arrive in her head.

Jeananne Kathol Kirwin is the author of the award-winning *Greetings from Cool Breezes* (Borealis Press, 2005). Her piece "Sundowners in the Cockpit" appears in the women's travel anthology *Outside of Ordinary* (Second Story Press, 2005), and her other travel writing has been shortlisted for the CBC Literary Awards. She lives in Edmonton with her husband and four children.

Deborah Lawson, a freelance editor and published non-fiction writer, has been a private poet since high school days. Four years ago she "went public" in Edmonton's charismatic and supportive poetry community, where the energy that comes from hanging out with other writers invigorates her own creative development. She enjoys experimenting with a variety of poetic forms. Poetry deepens her ability to engage with and pay attention to life, and allows her to be "at home" in a world where her affinity for words, metaphor and meaning is welcomed rather than considered peculiar. In 2007, one of Deborah's poems was chosen as Poetry Winner in the *Other Voices* 20th Anniversary Fiction, Non-Fiction and Poetry Contest.

Brenda Leifso's first book of poetry, *Daughters of Men*, is forthcoming from Brick Books in April, 2008.

Ian LeTourneau is a transplanted Maritimer. His poetry has appeared in numerous magazines and journals across the country, as well as CBC's Alberta Anthology. Gaspereau Press published a chapbook of his poems, *Defining Range*, in 2006. He lives in Athabasca with his wife, son and cat.

Carol L. MacKay lives in Bawlf, AB. Her poems have appeared in *The Fiddlehead*, *Antigonish Review*, *Prairie Journal*, *Lichen* and in *Threshold: An Anthology of Contemporary Writing from Alberta* (U of A Press, 1999). Her poem collection "Othala" was shortlisted for the 2004 CBC Literary Awards. She also writes for children.

Margaret Macpherson is a sometimes poet who is still adjusting to life in Alberta. She has published six books; four historic non fiction books, including a biography of Nellie

McClung, a collection of short stories entitled *Perilous Departures* and, late last year, her first novel *Released*.

Stuart Ian McKay is a member of the Writers Guild of Alberta and the League of Canadian Poets. *Stele of Several Ladies* – a long poem, his first book, was published in 2005. He is a two-time winner of CBC's Alberta Anthology and in 2006 participated in CBC's Poetry Face Off in Calgary. Stuart lives in Calgary where he is working on his second book, *a cognate of prayer*, a series of long poems about people with disabilities.

Catherine McLaughlin is a poet, photographer, freelance writer. Her artistic work is often informed by the natural world, especially the Peace River Country in northern Alberta where she has lived for more than 30 years. She has always felt most at home on the land and it continues to fascinate her. Catherine's poetry has been published in many publications and collections and twice she toured parts of central and southern Alberta, sharing her Peace Country poetry and photography. Her writing has attracted attention in several contests, including the People's Poetry Fall Contest (1999) and the Grande Prairie Public Library's poetry contest (2003).

Andy Michaelson "knocked around for a lot of years" and worked in broadcasting prior to launching his writing career in 1999. Along with a group of friends, he published a collection titled *Words Like Ashes* in 2007. Michaelson is currently working on a book of poetry and paintings about Norse and Aboriginal legends and history with Metis/First Nations painter Aaron Paqette, with help from former Senator Thelma Chalifoux.

Poet, translator, author of stories, essays and book reviews, **Anna Mioduchowska** has lived in Edmonton most of her life. Her most recent work appears in: *Edmonton on Location, River City Chronicles*, published by NeWest Press, *Writing the Terrain*, a poetry anthology, U of Calgary Press, and *Dance the Guns to Silence : 100 poems for Ken Saro Wiwa*, by Flipped Eye Publishing in London England. Her collection of poetry, *In-Between Season*, was published by Rowan Books.

Kerry Mulholland is a writer rooted in Alberta's soil, with loyalties divided between prairie, desert, city and sea. She has performed her poetry for audiences in teahouses, bookstores, jazz bars and under a tent in the rain at a music festival. Her work has been published in anthologies and periodicals and recorded on CDs. She was the winner of the Edmonton Journal's 2006 poetry contest, and winner of the Alberta 2007 CBC Radio Poetry Face-Off. Trained as a journalist, Kerry has worked as a writer for the provincial government, as a reporter for a small town newspaper, as a coordinator of women's writing workshops in Canada and New Mexico, as a bookbinder, as a typesetter, and as a program coordinator for the Writers Guild of Alberta. Always, words are near.

Ben Murray is an Edmonton-based writer whose poetry has appeared in many journals, including *Descant, Event, Grain, CV2, Queen's Quarterly*, and *The Windsor Review*. A debut poetry collection, *What We're Left With*, is forthcoming this fall from Brindle & Glass.

Blaine Newton is an Alberta playwright with productions across Western Canada and a total audience of well under a million people. His short fiction and poetry have been featured on CBC Radio and in the *Edmonton Journal*, and published in anthologies of Alberta writers. A founding member of the ACME Theatre Company ("Fine Theatre Since Tuesday"), writing and performing sketch comedy, he also contributed a regular humour column to Winnipeg's *Interchange Magazine*. Blaine works in Red Deer as an engineer as part of the writer-in-exile program.

Rob K. Omura lives in Calgary, Alberta, Canada where he practices law. He holds a BA in psychology and MA in history from the University of Calgary, and a LLB from Dalhousie University. He recently returned to his love of writing after a 15 year hiatus. He is active in education, law reform, the environment and the outdoors. His fiction and poetry appears or is forthcoming in *The Arabesques Review*, *Barnstorm*, *The Rose and Thorn*, *Agency*, *34th Parallel*, *Poems Niederngasse*, *edifice WRECKED* and *blue skies poetry*. He is currently working on a novel.

Catherine Owen's titles include: *Somatic – The Life and Work of Egon Schiele* (Exile Editions 1998), nominated for the Gerald Lampert Award, *The Wrecks of Eden* (Wolsak and Wynn, 2002), shortlisted for the BC Book Prize, *Shall: ghazals* (Wolsak and Wynn, 2006) and *Cusp/detritus* (Anvil Press, 2006), nominated for the ReLit Award. *Seeing Lessons* (2007) was recently shortlisted for the CBC Literary Awards. Her poems have been translated into Italian (*Caneide* with Joe Rosenblatt, 2005) and Korean. She plays bass/sings in the blackmetal band, INHUMAN. She's been writing about living in Edmonton since June 2006.

Paul Pearson lives and writes in Edmonton where he has been a member of the poetry community for almost two decades. Paul spent a number of years working for the Alberta Government and the Alberta Foundation for the Arts as the Writing and Publishing Consultant. Since moving on to other opportunities within government last year, Paul has re-discovered both the time and energy to write.

Susan Picard is youngest child of a northern Alberta farm family. She left home at 17 to pursue her dreams... a path that had her exploring different career possibilities: social worker, crisis counsellor, professional musician and teacher. At present she spends her time taking care of her family and utilizing her musical talents in creating unique community building events.

Pierrette Requier was raised in the village of Donnelly. Although she has spent most of her adult life in Alberta's capital city, she has always remained aware of having been fundamentally influenced and formed by having lived in the large spaces of the North where her grandparents on both sides came to settle as pioneers in the Peavine Creek area. She has regularly needed to return 'home' to all that flat space and the boreal forest for renewal and restoration, yet thinks that there is something that remains untamed and defies naming about thisland, thus writing the land always feels tentative, almost impossible, a larger than life task. Requier has been involved in the Edmonton Stroll of Poets Society for fifteen years, as well as the Tangent Lines spoken word group. She also facilitates Wind Eye Poetry Seminars.

Gayle Sacuta lives in Devon, Alberta. She spends her time exploring creativity by caring for her family (nurturing three boys, baking artisan bread), making fiber art (weaving, spinning and felting), playing and writing music (fiddle and guitar) and promoting literacy (kids song and story workshops, adult literacy programs).

Greg Schmidt lives in Beaverlodge with his family where he works as an electrician, meditates and writes poetry. "a prayer to peace" is his first published poem.

Bob Stallworthy has 2 self-published chapbooks and 3 full-length books of poetry published by a recognized publisher. The most recent book of poetry, *Optics*, Frontenac House 2004, was short-listed for the 2004 W.O. Mitchell City of Calgary Book Prize. *In Silhouette: Profiles of Alberta Writers*, a non-fiction e-book hosted on the Frontenac House website was launched in 2007. He is a Lifetime member of the Writers Guild of Alberta, a full member of the League of Canadian Poets and a member of the Young Alberta Book Society. His next manuscript is titled *Too Small for My Skin*.

Richard Stevenson teaches English and Creative Writing at Lethbridge College. Recent books include *Parrot With Tourette's* (Black Moss, Palm Poets Series, 2006), *Bye Bye Blackbird* (Ekstasis Editions, 2007) (both poetry titles), and *Riding on a Magpie Riff* (memoir, Settlements series, Black Moss Press, 2006). Two more haiku, senryu, zappai, and tanka books are forthcoming from Spotted Cow Press in Edmonton and Ekstasis Editions in Victoria.

Joanne Underwood currently lives in Alberta and enjoys going on day trips around the province. She's a member of the wordweavers writing collective, practising her poetry and entering CBC contests. Her latest successes have been with Shakespearean sonnets—one only for bragging rights and the other for a dual-flush toilet! Hoping her writing career is not really in the toilet, she continues to write for various contests, enjoying the stimulus of the subject at hand. She has had a haiku published in *Geist* magazine.

Tom Wayman currently teaches English and creative writing at the University of Calgary, after a long career teaching in mainstream and alternative post-secondary writing programs in B.C. In Winter 2007 he was the Fulbright Visiting Chair in Creative Writing at Arizona State University, and in October 2007 will hold the Ralph

Gustafson Chair in Poetry at Malaspina University-College, Nanaimo, B.C. His most recent books (2007) are a collection of poems, *High Speed Through Shoaling Water*, and a first collection of short fiction, *Boundary Country*. He is president of the board of Sheri-D Wilson's Calgary International Spoken Word Festival.

Audrey J. Whitson is the author of a critically acclaimed book about land and the spiritual journey, *Teaching Places* (Wilfrid Laurier University Press, 2003). She grew up on a farm north of Edmonton. This poem is from a series she did on the boreal forest.

About the Editors

Dymphny Dronyk, born in the Summer of Love in the City of Sin (Amsterdam, the Netherlands), is a writer, artist, mediator and mother. Passionate about the magic of story, she has woven words for money (journalism, corporate writing) and for love (poetry, fiction, drama, mystery novels) for over 25 years. After years of rambling on an eclectic career path (camp cook, editor, waitress, photographer), her gypsy spirit took root in the Peace Country and her energy is now directed towards raising her three children and running her business - Dynamic Data Complete Emergency Response Planning and Mediation.

Creatively, Dymphny has published articles, fiction and poetry in magazines and newspapers in Europe and in North America since 1984. She was the founder and publisher of *Between Gynes Magazine* in Victoria (1990-1992), and the co-editor of *Art of the Peace Magazine* (2003-2004). Dymphny has published poetry in Canadian anthologies: *Paperwork*, Harbour Press, 1991, ed. Tom Wayman; *Grain*, Saskatchewan Writers Guild, 1988; *Room of One's Own (Working for a Living)*, Growing Room Collective, ed.

Sandy Shreve; *Journey to the Interior*, (An Anthology of Kootenay Women Writers), Kimberley Writers Group, 1986, eds. Luanne Armstrong, Irene Mock, Paulette Jiles; *Nose Mountain Moods*, Smoky Peace Press, 2002, ed. Elroy Deimert. Her first volume of poetry *Contrary Infatuations*, was published by Frontenac House as part of Quartet 2007.

Angela Kublik descends from a long line of peasant farmers and serfs. She grew up on a farm 3 1/2 miles southeast of Barrhead in the house her grandparents built the year her father was born. Although she has lived in Edmonton, Grande Prairie and London, England, much of her writing continues to be inspired by the family farm where her parents still live and work. She currently resides in Edmonton and works as the Director of the Fort Saskatchewan Public Library. Her poetry has appeared in various venues, including *FreeFall, The Prairie Journal of Canadian Literature, DailyHaiku.Org* and, most recently, *Legacy*. She edits *blueskiespoetry.ca*, an online journal that provides a forum for emerging and established poets to find a wider audience for their work, with a particular emphasis on writing by Canadians.